Book One

SCHUMANN-SCHAUM

BASED ON EVENTS AND EPISODES OF SCHUMANN'S LIFE

The Purpose of the Schumann-Schaum Edition

Robert Schumann (1810–1856) was a central figure of musical Romanticism in Germany. His contributions are most significant in the fields of piano music and song. In this edition, Mr. Schaum has renamed some of Schumann's pieces with appealing titles that more accurately reflect the mood of the piece. Some of the compositions are purposely abridged, making them more accessible to the early-intermediate and intermediate-level student. The original titles and opus numbers are included for each piece. Featured in this collection are famous selections from *Album for the Young, Scenes From Childhood, Carnival,* and *Albumblätter* and arrangements of Schumann's Piano Quintet, Op. 44; Concerto in A minor, Op. 54; Symphonic Etudes, Op. 13; and "Larghetto" from *Spring Symphony.* Mr. Schaum's historically appropriate captions add color and life and the wealth of true biographical information adds musical appreciation to these authentic Schumann excerpts.

Teachers will be happy to note that this Schumann-Schaum book contains one or more examples of each musical form for which Schumann was famous.

Editor: Gail Lew
Production Coordinator: Karl Bork
Cover Illustration: Magdi Rodríguez
Cover Design: María A. Chenique

Contents

THE RIVER MULDE

Melody, Op. 68, No. 1*

Robert Schumann was born in Zwickau, Germany, a quiet town along the Mulde River. He began his piano lessons at the age of six from J. G. Kuntzsch, organist of St. Mary's Church, and in 1820 he entered the Zwickau Lyceum, where he remained for eight years. The record of his public appearances indicates that he showed considerable ability as a pianist from an early age.

*This piece is presented in its original form. Right-hand fingerings in measure 4 and left-hand fingerings in measure 8 are Schumann's own. All other fingerings are editorial.

EL00318A

KNOCKS ON THE KNUCKLES

Papillons, Op. 2, No. 8

The village organ and piano teacher Herr Kuntsch, with his lusty 1-2-3-4 and an occasional knock on the knuckles, started Robert Schumann on his musical career. Robert, the youngest of five children, attended a local private school in Zwickau. After taking part in a performance with his teacher, Schumann composed a Psalm setting for soprano, alto, piano, and orchestra written on plain paper that he had ruled by himself and was performed by his fellow students and some other young friends.

POETRY AND VERSE

Scherzino, Op. 26, No. 3

In addition to his musical abilities, the young Schumann showed equal if not greater literary ability. He educated himself by reading in his father's library and compiled an anthology of poems including a few of his own. He wanted to become a poet and in 1825 began writing a second book of his own verses.

DREAMING
Traumerei, Op. 15, No. 7

Schumann also dreamed of becoming a great pianist and composer. He attended a piano recital given by Ignaz Moscheles and it inspired him to study even harder. He gathered eight of his musical friends into a little orchestra, which he directed. He also played four-hand piano arrangements of symphonies by Beethoven, Haydn, and Mozart with a neighbor.

SCHOOLBOYS MARCHING

Soldier's March, Op. 68, No. 2

Schumann took a leading part in the founding of two schoolboy groups, one a secret society that cultivated fencing and the other a literary society for the study of German literature. His literary enthusiasm for Jean Paul had an overwhelming effect on his already flowery prose style, and his musical enthusiasm for Franz Schubert renewed his passionate dedication to composition.

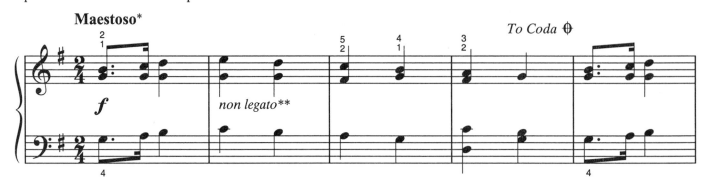

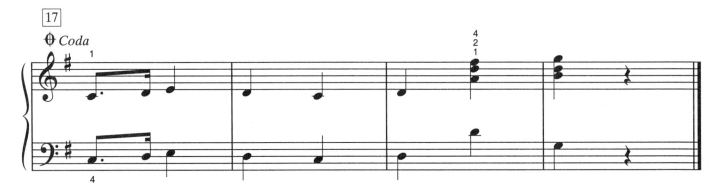

*Schumann's original tempo indication is Munter und straff (lively in a strict tempo).

**Schumann's original manuscript uses eighth notes followed by eighth rests. The editor uses non legato quarter notes for greater clarity and ease in reading.

EL00318A

HUMMING SONG

from Album for the Young, Op. 68, No. 3

After the death of his father, Schumann's mother took over responsibility for his education. She had her heart set on his becoming a lawyer and dismissed his musical and literary passion as nothing more than childish enthusiasm. After graduation, in obedience to his mother, he entered the University of Leipzig as a law student. Despite his promises to his mother that he would devote himself to legal study, he cut classes and spent hours daily on his imitations of Jean Paul and in improvisation at the piano.

*Schumann's original tempo indication is Nicht schnell (not fast).

EL00318A

THE DAVID CLUB

"Marche des 'Davidsbündler' contre le Philistins" from Carnival, Op. 9

In 1833 Schumann helped organize a musical society called the Davidsbündler (David Club). Just as David had attacked and defeated the Philistines, so these young Davids aspired to shatter bad music and raise the banner of high ideals and standards. Next, Robert started a magazine for the club to spread their ideas. The first issue of *The New Magazine for Music* appeared in 1834. With Schumann as editor, it became one of the finest journals of its kind in the world, a powerful influence in German music.

LITTLE SCENE ON FOUR NOTES

"Florestan" from Carnival, Op. 9

Schumann desperately tried to persuade his mother to allow him to abandon law for music as a profession. Friedrich Wieck told his mother that within three years he could make Schumann into one of the foremost living pianists provided he would work hard and steadily at piano technic and theory. His mother consented to a trial period of six months, and Schumann went to live in Wieck's own house to study and devote himself totally to music.

FIRST LOSS

from Album for the Young, Op. 68, No. 16

Professor Wieck, with whom Schumann lived while studying music, had a musically gifted daughter, Clara, much younger than Robert. Clara had begun her concert career, under her father's direction, when she was ten years old. Schumann admired her ability to perform, while she marveled at his written compositions and inventive games.

SPRING SYMPHONY

"Larghetto" from Symphony No. 1

One day, Schumann went to visit the brother of Franz Schubert. While he was there, he found many of Schubert's manuscripts, including that of the "Great" C major Symphony. This visit possibly inspired Schumann to sketch out his own symphony. Schumann's first ambitious work for orchestra is known as the *Spring Symphony*. The symphony was rehearsed by Felix Mendelssohn and performed under his direction at a concert given by Clara on behalf of the orchestra's pension fund.

SPRING NIGHT

Op. 39, No. 12

Clara was sixteen and Robert was twenty-five when they realized they were in love. Clara was about to leave with her father for a concert tour, and Robert came to say good-by. As Schumann turned to say a last farewell, he kissed Clara. That kiss started their long and eventful romance.

WHY?

"Warum" from Fantasiestücke, Op. 12, No. 3

Friedrich Wieck had no intention of encouraging a relationship between his daughter and Schumann. He forbade Clara to see or write to Schumann and sent her off to Dresden. Certainly Schumann must have asked himself, "Why?" Despite the distance between them, they never lost their determination to someday get married.

MUSICAL SPELLING
"Northern Song" from Album for the Young, Op. 68, No. 40

Schumann wrote a composition for the Countess Pauline Abegg by translating the letters of her name into the musical notes A, B, E, G, and G and made up a theme out of those notes. Niels Gade, another composer, gave the theme below to Schumann. The first four notes spell the name G, A, D, E.

THE INJURED HAND

"The Wild Horseman" from Album for the Young, Op. 68, No. 8*

In his goal to master the piano, Schumann devised a new method for making his fourth finger as flexible as the others. He invented a gadget of strings and leather that he wore around his hands. This artificial position did nothing to bring on flexibility, and he realized that his fingers were weakening instead of getting stronger. The gadget induced paralysis, and doctors could do nothing to relieve the condition. Thus, Schumann made the transition from pianist to composer.

*This piece is presented in its original form with editorial fingering.

EL00318A

THE VICTORIOUS LAWSUIT

from Symphonic Etudes, Op. 13, No. 12

Schumann brought a lawsuit against Friedrich Wieck to compel him legally to permit his marriage with Clara to take place. After six stormy years of courtship and many trying months of trial, Clara and Robert were married at the village church of Schoenfeld near Leipzig.

Allegro brillante

CRADLE SONG

from Albumbläutter, Op. 124, No. 6

In August 1841 Clara tried out Schumann's new *Fantasie in A minor* for piano and orchestra at a rehearsal. Two weeks later she gave birth to Marie, the first of their eight children. Schumann wrote two albums of piano pieces for children. When Clara made the comment to her husband that in many ways he resembled a child, he wrote *Scenes from Childhood*. Later he wrote *Album for the Young* about subjects close to the hearts of children.

COMMAND PERFORMANCE

from Arabeske, Op. 18

From the time she was ten years old, Clara Schumann had appeared at the largest concert halls in Europe. As one of the most famous pianists of her time and one of the great stars of nineteenth-century musical Europe, she premiered many new works by Frédéric Chopin, Johannes Brahms, and her husband, Robert Schumann. She performed in the salons of Leipzig's rich and famous and made concert tours to Dresden, Paris, Berlin, and Vienna.

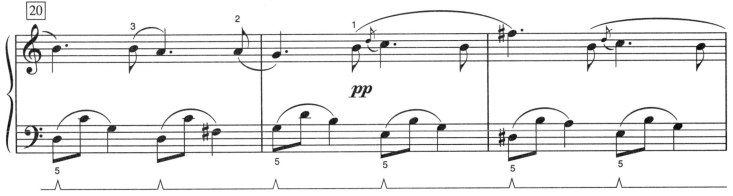

REAPER'S SONG

from Album for the Young, Op. 68, No. 18

Toward the end of his career, Schumann experienced strong and painful ringing sounds in his head. One night he awoke and wrote down a theme in E♭, which he said the angels had sung to him. The next two nights he said that the angels were gone and in their place were tigers and hyenas that threatened him. He was so upset that he ran out of the house to the Rhine Bridge and jumped in the river. He was rescued by some fishermen and brought home.

Allegro ma non troppo

*An eight measure section of unison eighth notes was omitted between measures 12 and 13. The rest of the piece appears in its original form.

EL00318A

THE HAPPY FARMER

from Album for the Young, Op. 68, No. 10

Schumann was active as a musical journalist from 1831 to 1844. He loved to conceal himself behind the fictional characters of Florestan and Eusebius. He also gave names to the members of the Davidsbündler (David Club) to conceal the identity of the real people.

Animato e grazioso*

*Schumann's original tempo indication is Frisch und munter (lively and fresh).

EL00318A

WEDDING ANNIVERSARY

from Piano Quintet, Op. 44

Even with the responsibility of eight children to raise, Clara continued to give concerts and Robert continued to compose. Every wedding anniversary was celebrated with a gift of music from Robert to Clara.

FESTIVAL CONCERTO

Piano Concerto in A minor, Op. 54

By 1854 Schumann's complaints of pain and depression were worse. He asked to be placed in a mental hospital, where he died two years later. After his death, Clara continued to perform his music. The climax of her musical career came when she played an all-Schumann recital at the Schumann Festival in Bonn, Germany. Today Schumann's music is performed and loved throughout the world.

I. First Movement

Allegro brillante

II. Second Movement

III. Third Movement

Allegro vivace

John W. Schaum
(1905–1988)

Founder and director of the Schaum Music School in Milwaukee, Wisconsin, John W. Schaum is the composer of internationally famous piano teaching materials including more than 200 books and 450 sheet music pieces. He is author of the internationally acclaimed *Schaum Piano Course* published by Belwin-Mills Publishing Corporation/Warner Bros. Publications. During his extensive travels, Mr. Schaum presented hundreds of piano teacher workshops in all fifty states. He was president of the Wisconsin Music Teachers Association and soloist with the Milwaukee Philharmonic Orchestra.

Mr. Schaum received a master of music degree from Northwestern University, a bachelor of music degree from Marquette University, and a bachelor of music education degree from the University of Wisconsin-Milwaukee.

He remains an important influence in the lives of hundreds of thousands of piano students who have enjoyed and continue to play his music.